# O Death

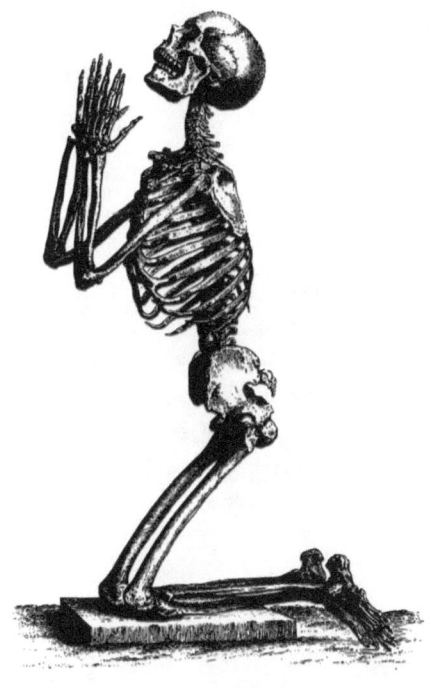

Poems by Justin Hamm

Spartan
Press

# Spartan Press

Kansas City, Missouri

Copyright ©Justin Hamm, 2024

First Edition: 1 3 5 7 9 10 8 6 4 2

ISBN: 978-1-958182-84-0

LCCN: 2024943829

Cover and title page images: Public domain

Author photo: Mel Hamm

# Acknowledgments

Some of these poems first appeared in the following journals:

"Prayer to the Absent Father:" *San Pedro River Review,*
"Multiverses:" *Unbroken,* "Banjo Frogs:" *Laurel Review,*
"I always keep an eye out for those places:" *Laurel Review,*
"I wasn't going to do one on Fentanyl:" *Laurel Review,*
"Like a horse whipped:" *Cobalt Weekly,* "What Could That
Be:" *Ran Away with the Star Bassoon,* "in the cold furnace:"
*Unlost,* "Why?:" *Heavy Feather Review,* "You get to forty, and
suddenly:" *Belt Magazine,* "a lonely girl," "Heroes eat nothing:"
*Gasconade Review*


Special thanks to John Dorsey, Jason Ryberg, John Gallaher,
Marybeth Neiderkorn, Al Maginnis, Justin Evans, Michael
Meyerhofer, Gary McDowell, and Jeff Newberry for
comments and support.

# Table of Contents

come down The man said  /  1

Prayer to the Absent Father  /  5

If a Crow Happens to Land Anywhere

   the Grass is Green  /  6

Everywhere the river is wide  /  8

You get to forty and suddenly  /  9

the kind bones of poverty  /  10

Multiverses  /  11

a lonely girl  /  12

Secret Boy  /  13

no peace till hell  /  14

Banjo Frogs  /  16

Like a horse whipped  /  17

Variations on Three Questions from Quora  /  19

I ain't no Papa  /  27

Hand on the Plow  /  31

O grizzled rotted Americans  /  32

Communion  /  33

of the bizarre  /  37

What Could That Be?  /  38

the theme of death  /  41

Why?  /  43

i oft wonder  /  45

I always keep an eye out for those places  /  46

In the cold furnace  /  47

I Wasn't Going to do One on Fentanyl  /  48

Lucifer  /  49

O Death  /  50

Heroes eat nothing  /  53

Composed to Jelly Roll Morton's
    "Hyena Stomp"  /  54

The plunge into death Having failed  /  55

I ambled out one morning  /  56

look here  /  61

He slept in a one-room cabin  /  62

into the wastebasket with me  /  65

For the poets, all of you, known and unknown,
who toil to keep verse alive.

*"Now Death, o Death, consider my age*
*and do not take me at this stage.*
*My wealth is all at your command*
*if you will move your icy hand.*

*The old, the young, the rich, the poor,*
*they alike with me will have to go.*
*No age, no wealth, no silver, no gold,*
*nothing satisfies me but your poor soul."*

From the traditional folk song "Conversations
with Death," first attributed to Lloyd Chandler

come              d own

The man said


          Lord

Lord, Lord

come          d own



   nobody home                    no one to be  found




          from "High Water Everywhere Part II"
          by Charley Patton

## Prayer to the Absent Father

Dear Lord of the loose dirt
under my fingernails,

both maker and healer
of leaky heart valves.

Dear keeper of the secret
meaning of birdsong

and unseen ringer
of all distant bells.

Namer of names, scatterer
of rain over cornstalks.

Blesser of potlucks and myriad
gravies of the great Midwest.

Dear knower of what we are
apparently never to know,

You, Who by definition
has so many virtues.

Tell me why it always seems
listening isn't one.

## If a Crow Happens to Land Anywhere the Grass is Green

I couldn't really say what depressed him he just liked
to lay back there in the dark bedroom with the air
conditioning on and listen to old-time country and
church songs from out of the hills that birthed him
he didn't talk to anyone in those days it kept him from
taking a gun to his temple or baptizing a hundred
pills in whiskey again like he did that summer I was
thirteen I had to call emergency I had never imagined
he might want to die he always seemed so wise in his
slightly broken way even though I guess those two
things could still go together later I fell for hank and
the carter family and a little of the drink and depression
myself but a remarkable woman and our babies cured
me sometimes I will visit and if there's nobody around
sing keep on the sunny side at his grave which is right
next to my mother's grave in that cemetery beside the
hayfield if a crow happens to land anywhere the grass is
green or the wind shakes the old juniper a certain way I
imagine he is finally a part of the music itself now and
it's a comfort to think these trials of the flesh are no
longer his concern

Everywhere

the river is wide


                                    and

difficulties

never lie still


Nine times in ten you can't

see where                           the


devils have swapped                 course




from Mark Twain's *Life on the Mississippi*

# You get to forty, and suddenly

there is in direct lockstep beside you a fairly serious-
seeming man skin gray-washed as winter morning a man
who is always with you and who insists he can see into
the secret cave of tears you hide inside your gut that lair
where once the air was a gallery of her breath you say it
out loud and whistle forty! forty and alive in a city where
yardkept children on swingsets swear slurs against each
other's mothers while traffic lights the city's moodrings
blink and shift and blink you step the man steps you step
et cetera over a dead man's shuttered coffee shop an icy
mist begins to fall the friend you did not choose gestures
and declares all memories after this age are steel rooms
in need of ventilation he promises if you put down
your club he can resurrect any dead horse it's an offer
to consider naturally the last remaining drops of human
inside you feel tempted to sidestep any prophet blowing
smoke from a cheap cigar but you are lonely and this one
at least remembered to bring a sensible hat

the kind


                                        bones of poverty
contain              forty-thousand


streets
with
        houses
to pile up their

    solemn                              pioneer
history

immigrant,          ax          hoe



from Mark Twain's *Life on the Mississippi*

*Multiverses*

I don't fully understand the intricacies but I believe there
exist parallel to this poem an infinite number of other
poems that twist and turn in nearly inconceivable ways
in one for instance politicians sit together over dinner
and come to reasonable compromises that benefit a
large majority of their constituents in another instead of
bones and meat and blood and systems the people are
filled with a harsh dry wind a few stray autumn leaves
scraping through their chests there is a poem in which
your lover has not moved to Nebraska with a rough-
jawed younger man you still enjoy sitting together on the
porch each morning sipping black coffee and taking in
the expanse of the mountain view just as there is a
poem in which your lover is dying something to do
with the liver and you perch like Lady Margaret at his
bedside and puzzle together a future you'll never want
there are thousands of poems ruled over by benevolent
magicians and just as many in which silence is the prime
form of language and words are what get said to avoid
having to actually say anything and you and I it seems
we are bound exclusively to this poem where the air
smells like the air of your present location the coffee
has stained my teeth more than I care to accept and our
memories sound like forgotten folksongs playing in the
room across the hall

A lonely girl

          in a copper boat

fashions a long rope

      of the     moon


   but        she does not open

her eyes



ever

from "The Process of Individuation," M. L. von Franz. *Man and His Symbols* edited by Carl G. Jung

*Secret Boy*

We lost you that August back to school sales slow slur of baseball broadcasts wildflower clusters like paint spilled over brown Missouri prairie there were so many people to call your sisters had only just forgiven us and decided you might fit in there were naming wars in the evenings side-eye declarations of who you would favor most (of course it would have been me) it is never anything good when the doctor leads with I'm sorry words that can actually be seen trailing from slow-motion mouth even softly spoken even tenderly intended still arcing with menace toward unready ears how many times have you been born since that day incubated in the shelter of my imagination milkfed by your mother's wish memory A and S sometimes glance down as we pose for family portraits we know they wonder I mourn you in wild children's stories like those I improvised when A and S were small ukulele ringing minor chords voice rising and falling a preacher a Sesame Street preacher I give my stories to students in the library now choosing the best behaved as main characters I wish just once I could see your eyes astonished as I reveal near the end you are the secret brave one you are the one who returns through hidden trapdoor it is you who visits the cobwebby dark underneath and returns fists full of everything that was taken

No peace till
                    hell
              no job

No
        potatoes

Go down to the water
Go on now


ain't much light      and


              you ain't clean



from John Steinbeck's *The Grapes of Wrath*

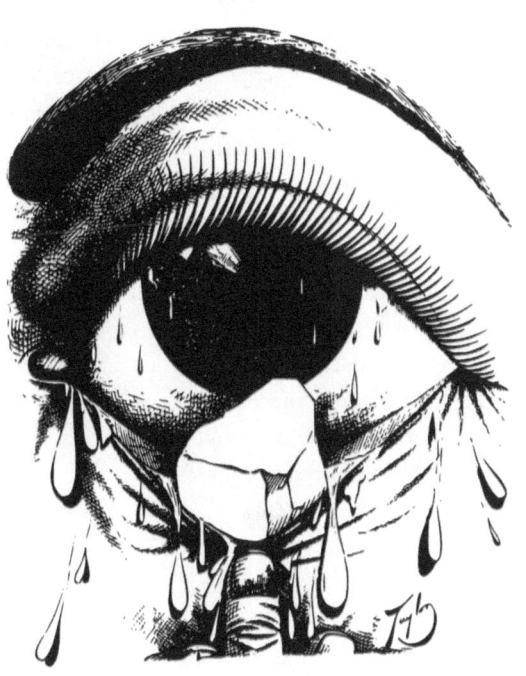

## Banjo Frogs

In southeastern Australia frogs carry their banjos in their throats here in America we force them to spend much of their ten-year lifespan learning to play with webbed toes so our folk artists might affix them to t-shirts and bolo ties of quaint Appalachian chic appeal we Americans love for our animals to perform human tricks this is why our elephants can paint landscapes and our dogs can operate the same electronic tablets as our children it is also why some of our legislators have learned to spell and even sign their own names which they only do when it enriches themselves or inflicts social and financial harm on others I'll be honest I don't always recognize this land around me anymore and I am not especially old sometimes in the summer I sit outside on the porch and pick out the first part of dueling banjos again and again to myself it is the only part of the song I could ever master it used to be a source of some embarrassment these strange days it seems like more than enough to drive home the point

Like a

horse    whipped

  amid a chorus of laughter

A woman        standing the near the top

in the shadow

          of her                    shadow

from James Joyce's "The Dead," *Dubliners*

*Variations on Three Questions from Quora*
*with apologies to Pablo Neruda*

*What do you think happens when you close your eyes for the last time on earth does everything go black immediately?* is it no longer necessary to grind your teeth to refrain from constant sobbing are the loveletters in your dresser drawer addressed to someone who is not your partner no longer a source of any concern can a coffin float if there happens to be a great flood on the day of your interment are you okay if a few flies land on your forehead now that you can longer feel someone said every hundred years there are all new people on earth would you mind too much if the organs you marked for donation were instead transformed into a new kind of art

*What happens if you don't get a tetanus shot after getting cut with rusty metal?* does your blood turn to an Appalachian dirt road do tiny bootleggers run shine through your veins can you tune yourself in to border radio stations are you your own churning factory now can you set a swinging pendulum to the pace of the word oxidation do you believe you still need fluoride in your drinking water are the crows in the barnloft like your sisters and brothers would you prefer pictures of saints or soldiers on your adhesive bandages can you forgive your mother and father their corroded marriage is it possible to paint the shape of glory with your fingertips does your jaw feel a bit stiff and underappreciated doesn't blood already taste like metal at least that's what I believe I heard

*If electricity comes from electrons, does morality come from morons?* does throwing the dice or the bones determine our outlook does it feel better to scream in small circles or all together as one does drinking wine expand vocabulary shall we pretend to love what does not love us in return does Saturday sound okay or would Sunday be better does levity come from wearing Levi's does felicity come from herding felines does duality arise from the desire to stand before another in anger and try to remove their heart with a sword or do I have my homophones crossed

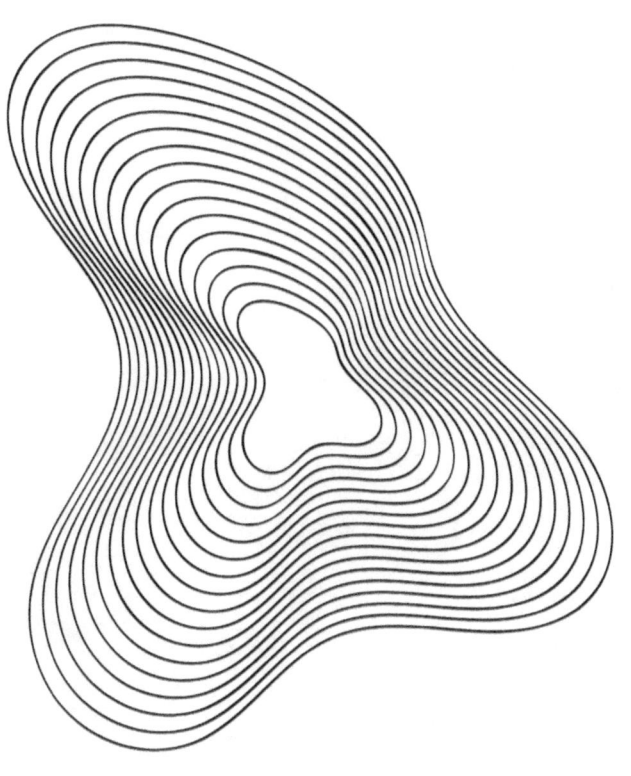

I ain't      no

              Papa
     on       no
Freight train


i  don't do
sorrow

     I         ring


Lord      bring
     me       your brand new   ear




from "34 Blues" by Charley Patton

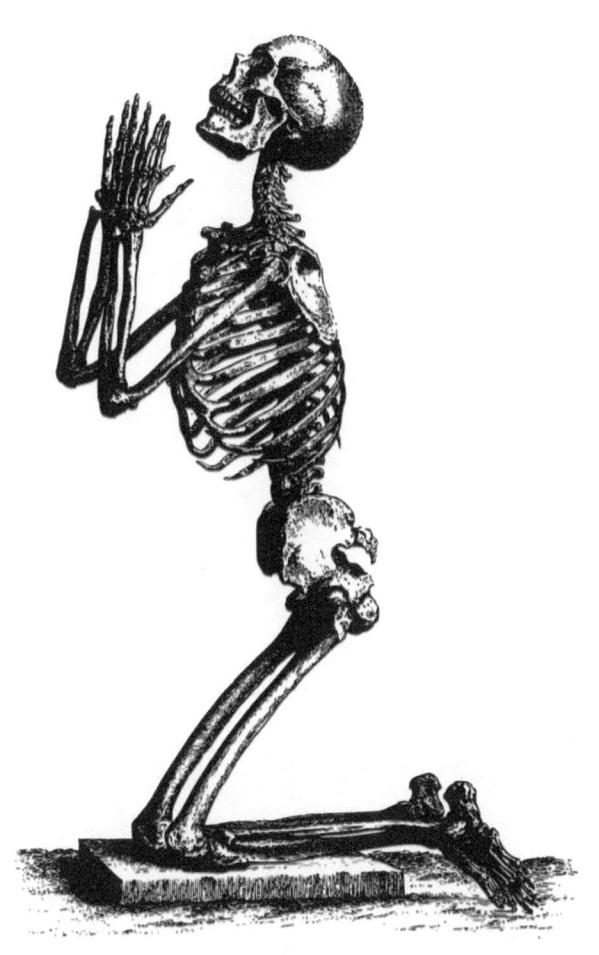

*Hand On The Plow*

keep the real news in a locket near your heart attack a white lead lie loaded in every chamber keep your bacon grease in a jar near the stovetop keep your Nietzsche in the back of the deep freeze your Dali mustache as thin as a cigarette be neither cruel nor rude nor ever stingy but keep the better hallelujahs for yourself keep good time but do not bend to it keep a candle flickering in every window and for God's sake don't forget to leave the back door ajar *Matthew, Mark, Luke, and John all those prophets dead and gone keep your hand on the plow and hold on*

O
grizzled
rotted

Americans
who have suffered



money     will   be     our

new Angel        of




peace


from *The Autobiography of Mark Twain*

# Communion

*for John Dorsey, Jason Ryberg,* and *Abraham Smith*

Late night sweat-soaked Ozarks so dark unclear if we have
even been born four chairs four porch-sitting poets room in
the center for the holy spirit to stretch out and hum in the
blackforest distance the Gasconade ancient muddy home to
drowned-rat seraph and wide-eyed bass rainswollen raging
her way home to her Missouri River mouth there comes a
rare passage of headlights near the road the faintest myth
of civilization a laugh a cough a laugh a short silence before
someone in sneakers speaks in tongues of fire a lonesome
armadillo scuttles into a small circle of moonlight to
give birth to the first mystery someone says Wordsworth
Quixote Townes Van Zandt someone else says cancer
someone passes me a stringed instrument and an open
bottle of beer

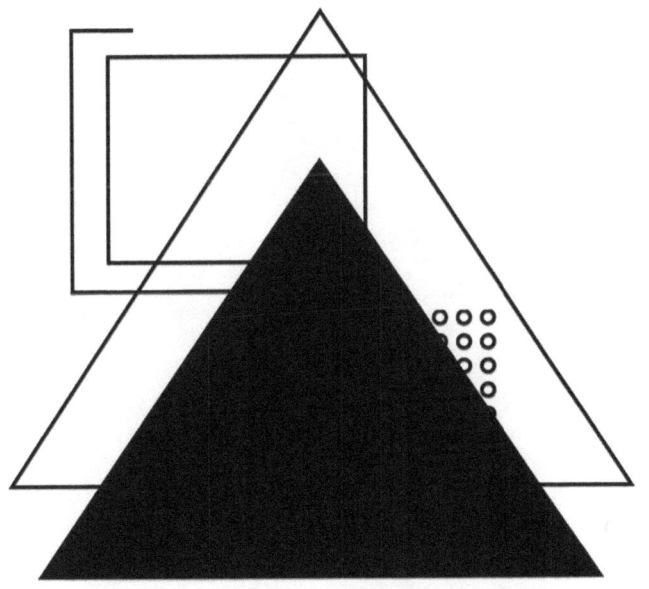

                                        of the

bizarre

            of

the            wild

                        velvet



                        of

the dreams        and

the tripods

and

                                    the blood-colored

ears

of        the clock


        the last chime            sunk into silence


                    And        rumor



        from Edgar Allan Poe's
        "The Masque of the Red Death"

## What Could That Be?

It could be the sound of whatever animal a woman carries in her heart tearing through her chest tattoo pacing growling sniffing behind the ears of your inside animal or else the sound of fallen lightning turning to fire across a field a fire of desperation or invitation maybe the sound of your special medication speaking shyly to her special medication or the wet tones of one bank account weeping as another bank account shudders or pages turning in an empty ledger the family bible a notebook of prairie haiku scrawled in blue crayon it's hard to say it could be a broken farewell to a farmhouse the sizzle of an ancient corn crib baking in the summer heat a tomb of old maize magic so strong once large voodoo men of straw were crucified just to keep away the dark clouds of crows crow mouths you see being wholly unsuited to the silence expected of human grief

the theme of death

causes

oracles

to point

at

coincidences, and make them


terrible

as if they are

spectator sports


from "The Process of Individuation,"
M. L. von Franz. *Man and His Symbols*
edited by Carl G. Jung

# Why?

There's a boy who beats an invisible drum and a boy who loves nothing more than to stand in the weeds and to run his fingers over the rough wood of the neighbor's barn and a boy who hides from his chores and a boy who wants to parlay with his own confusion and that boy stands here in those weeds now with his eyes closed and the barnwood is splintery the sun on his face and there's something here to be known and felt it lives inside the wood a story maybe or a special secret and no he isn't going to catch any fish and no he isn't going to learn to use the guns his cousins caress like pretty girls remember how they laughed when he was almost crushed by the delivery truck he only wanted to help the turtle why did it bite and why is blood red anyway and why does it burn sometimes in the chest or the stomach to think about certain people and why do pigs roll around in their own muck and the old woman his grandmother why does she prefer him to all the rest  make him sit near her and hold her cracked and crooked hands and listen to her cough through those moldy old songs by the fire her quilts she calls them says they're sewn together with hope and broken notes what is the barnwood trying to tell us that trees don't bleed the pigs do when you stick them the clouds bleed sort of if you think of rain that way Jesus bled he sure did! and they say he's coming back too but why after all that was done to him and why would the pigs even want to be born when you think of it if we're only going to stick them and why would people even want to be born if all that happens is it burns this way to think about them everyone on fire inside as they think about each other their guns and their fried fish their better and worse clothes and how they swing laughter down like hammers and how clowns dress up with their paint-on smiles as if naked frowns aren't allowed why can't you just frown if it's a world that makes you frown or scowl or cry and why can't you just stop here if you want and feel the rough wood of a barn and listen to the insects and count your breaths in your own head which is just like praying if you think about it without somebody saying okay Weirdo it's time to move along or yelling at you or asking you to just come inside for a minute don't be afraid it's just for a minute when inside is someplace you know you really shouldn't go

i        oft        wonder
Why

the sunshine
    leaves


 why
the sunshine
seem  s nothing

                    why
        the sunshine
is
                all
    alon   e
                in the
by and by




        from the early 20th century hymn
        "Farther Along," as sung  by Mississippi
        John Hurt

*I always keep an eye out for those places*

where the darkness hides walk-in closets glove compartments the hard stare of a man in a watchman's cap buying dog food and drill bits at the feed store you would think I would finally learn to live with it always nearby the snarling darkness that could eat up everything to live with it the way we all live knowing certain neighbors have tupperware containers of ammunition bizarre justifications scrawled between versus in Ezekial and Deuteronomy but I never do you just have to get on the best you can we're told you just have to feel good about the bees who still come around and forget about all the dead ones dead bees dead sisters dead uncles dead of war chewed up by worms and casket darkness dirt of grave darkness fat worms smoking big cigars in skull parlors in chambers of commerce chambers of congress no light in the slimy ones' eyes no light beneath their hats impossible to see the smoke the debauchery in their hotel rooms of hedonism if it is turtles really turtles all the way down you would never know it it wouldn't even matter it's too dark to see them anyway straining under such a load barred even from a sliver of cake on oblivion's birthday

                    In the cold
furnace
   the man
could                    hear
   joy          from
stars
   illuminated


He longed to be alone


                  alone


in his voice


        from James Joyce's "The Dead," *Dubliners*

## I wasn't going to do one on Fentanyl

just picture my mother in heavy makeup singing 90s country music Sawyer Brown oh some girls do bigged up bangs classic camaro baby blue it was a life she lived a life smoked two hundred million cigarettes I think she wanted me to be better off but not too better off didn't want me to become like respectable people they closed off other folks with their judgment and hatred that's what she thought of me that's what she thought I became bald and respectable and goddamn it I don't know if its true

Lucifer

looked at

modern art

in the negative

it must

value

nothing

h  e

formulated

human need

has become

lost

from "Symbolism in the Visual Arts,"
Aniela Jaffe. Man and His Symbols edited
by Carl G. Jung

## O Death

the truth of our limited breathing is nothing we want
to encounter too much like coming around a bend on a
hiking trail to find a man openly pissing  we try to avert
our eyes but there it is all revealed life as single night one
lightless stretch all of us feigning wakefulness tuning in
and out to the varied cricket-and-bass-toad orchestras
of handheld devices spilled-gravy cursewords clumsy
declarations of matters internal to our heartmeat which
never quite matches with anyone else's heartmeat the only
trick I have learned is to treat it all like lucid dreaming
to morph each moment bend each brittle experience
with real-time nostalgia on a riding mower early 1980s
imagine you a child your grandfather's lap you slaughter by
helicopter blade a litter of bunnies an accident you might
sob it was an accident don't do that learn nothing from
the blood take no lesson about death or the inventory in
the old bastard's butcher shop only recall the two days
of scruff on your grandfather's face white like tiny sugar
granules as he pulls you close kills the mower covers your
eyes with his hands hums a melody rescued from the old
hill country where his infant eyes first squinted in the
sunlight at noon

Heroes            eat  nothing

                  ravens

                  feast                     on

Thought and Memory

                                            a poet


              upon men as well as

the gods




              from Edith Hamilton's *Mythology*

*Composed to Jelly Roll Morton's "Hyena Stomp"*

I met a hyena the color of dry earth he told me there were many roads to where I wished to go it seemed encouraging so why was he laughing why were his teeth cutting a wide slit through his face then I saw the roads the pock-marks the overgrowth downed electrical lines some with no shoulders with sheer dropoffs vanishing points of no light others crowded by roadside memorials and wayside shrines to ancestor dreamers the general idea of all this being you can't get there from here can't get anywhere from anywhere but after a minute this hyena points to another road there's a shaded canopy water coolers all along the way the pavement looks brand new it's very convenient I can see this is where he wants me to go I'm not going there I say why not says the hyena because that's where you want me to go I say I've always been like that you can ask my third grade teacher Mrs. Keune though I guess she's probably dead I say I'm only going where I want to go what are you gonna do then says the hyena go up one of them other roads you can't even pass I say no I'm going to stand right here and not go anywhere oh you're gonna stand right there and not go anywhere he says that's right I say he starts laughing again that's great that's too perfect he says just stay right there I mean that is just as good

                              The plunge into

                   death                    Having failed

I half smiled


then      fell suddenly calm


                   as if

                              the human

                                    remnant which had
been      me
 had
hope
of joy



                   I was an imbecile          an idiot


of the heart




                   from "The Pit and the Pendulum"
                   by Edgar Allan Poe

# I ambled out one morning

dressed in tweed jacket and stetson hat boy oh boy was
my beard freshly trimmed was my head clean and bald as
a bare light bulb beneath that soft american felt my brim
snapped up the red tailed hawks circling over a field where
rats waited in secret nests for precise time to storm nearby
houses seeking warmth a fine day I tell you I felt fine even
if my blood sugar was over two hundred and twenty again
even if my triglycerides had come back too high to measure
my mood was a wide-grinning Norman Blake tune though
come to think of it might not hurt to ramp up the pace
of this particular amble get the heartrate going like the
doctor says I'm supposed to but hey I have been writing
more poems lately keeping the machine of my ethical being
well-oiled staying in better contact with all these beautiful
friends I don't deserve calling the old man out of the blue
plus a bunch of people at work nominated me for employee
of the month I'm decent is what I'm saying here a decent
man but who knew decency wouldn't do shit for bad
cholesterol fatty liver here's the thing if I do keel over from
a heart attack my mom had two my dad had three my uncle
had two one grandfather died of a heart attack the other
survived three with open heart surgery scar like gnarled tree
roots down the middle of his chest even if that happens to
me I had good sense not long ago to up my life insurance
more than M and the girls could ever need I try to give
them something of myself to outlast me it's hard to wake
in the mornings see that tweed jacket and stetson resting
on a chair in the office thinking this will be all that remains
of me my style but no substance no more cornball jokes
on roadtrips no more sitting up with A trying to help her
understand how to coexist with the ultra-religious an hour

past bedtime no middle-aged man crying in the audience when S dances on stage just a coat and a hat both of fine materials scottish wool american felt both made to outlive the heart that beats in my chest by five lifetimes

              look here

    Now    look here


troubles


you

work                              night and day

                          both night and day




work


          for me

                    for

                                              my

                                        cause  to



                                        b




          from "When the Levee Breaks" by
          Kansas Joe McCoy and Memphis Minnie

*He slept in a one-room cabin*

deep in the woods that night windows open wide to the
gospel of spring air which should have been glorious
beneath three blankets but the lock on the front door
had rusted out over time and he came to sleep uneasily
and it was no surprise when the nightmares arrived but
instead of a murderer or even a wayward meth addict
with a stolen crowbar crashing into the darkness with
a Nicholsonian grin anxiety produced an even more
terrible film a live shooter at the elementary school where
he worked the godawful drumbeats of gunshots the
alarm and the garbled instructions over the automated
intercom as he rushed twenty-two tiny panicked bodies
into a storage closet the size of a half bath only to realize
he'd forgotten the class roster though he counted and
counted he could not remember everyone's name gagging
on stomach acid trying gently to shush a crier whose
face he couldn't see once he turned out the lights there
were hands on his legs tiny hands grabbing at his hands
shuffling sounds in the corner and something falling from
a shelf he tried to tether himself to time but could not
keep from thinking of his youngest daughter upstairs
in the fourth grade room the ancient door and wide
window such slight barriers between her and whatever
desperately wanted return them to the Earth as dust fear
with its ruthless intelligence playing chess while everyone
else was so busy always trying to jump over top of their
allies' checkers then morning the heartpound the sweat
the coffee and a question how many others have this
same dream behind doors locked or unlocked in town or
out in the woods each night in the miraculous country of
limitless Little Debbie snacks the very first country in the
world to put a human on the moon

into the wastebasket

with me


I could not                 consent

        to        Their book


I could not  allow myself

      to be

a member         when Providence

            was easily found to


crack


from *The Autobiography of Mark Twain*

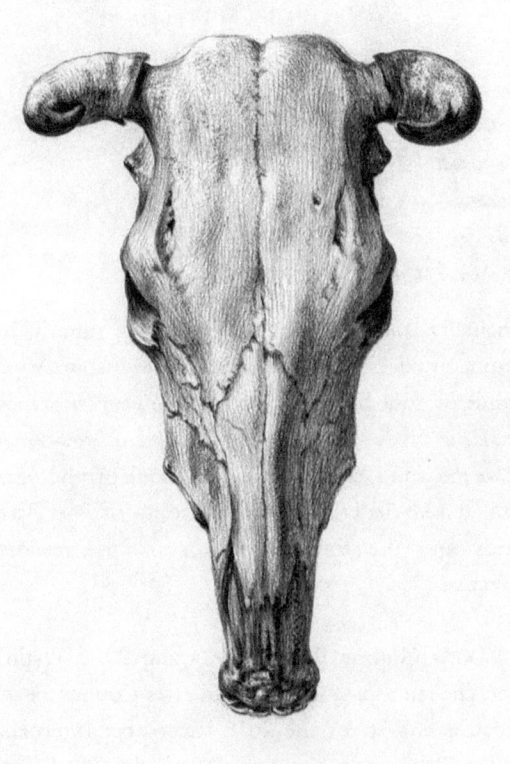

Originally from the flatlands of central Illinois, Justin Hamm now lives near Twain territory in Missouri. He is the author of four books of poetry, *Drinking Guinness With the Dead: Poems 2007-2021*, *The Inheritance*, *American Ephemeral*, and *Lessons in Ruin*, and a book of photographs entitled *Midwestern*. He is also the creator of Poet Baseball Cards and the founding editor of the *museum of americana*.

A Woody Guthrie Poet in 2024 and 2022, Justin has been chosen as a 2020 Missouri Arts Council Featured Artist, a finalist for the 2018 River Styx International Poetry Prize, and the winner of the 2014 Stanley Hanks Memorial Poetry Prize. In 2022 he delivered a performance entitled "The American Midwest: a Story in Poems" at TEDx Oshkosh. The recording can be viewed on YouTube. In 2019, Justin's poem "Goodbye, Sancho Panza" was studied by approximately 50,000 students worldwide as a part of the World Scholar's Cup curriculum.

Justin's individual poems, stories, photographs, collages, and reviews have appeared in *Nimrod International Journal*, *The Midwest Quarterly*, *Sugar House Review*, *Verse Daily*, *Southern Indiana Review*, *the New Poetry from the Midwest* anthology series, and many other publications. Additionally, his award-winning photographs have featured in numerous solo gallery shows. His poetry/photography hybrid exhibition "Midwestern" traveled the Midwest region from 2018-2020.

This project was made possible, in part, by generous support from the Osage Arts Community.

Osage Arts Community provides temporary time, space and support for the creation of new artistic works in a retreat format, serving creative people of all kinds — visual artists, composers, poets, fiction and nonfiction writers. Located on a 152-acre farm in an isolated rural mountainside setting in Central Missouri and bordered by ¾ of a mile of the Gasconade River, OAC provides residencies to those working alone, as well as welcoming collaborative teams, offering living space and workspace in a country environment to emerging and mid-career artists. For more information, visit us at www.osageac.org

Osage Arts Community

www.ingramcontent.com/pod-product-compliance
Lightning Source LLC
Chambersburg PA
CBHW031248120626
46545CB00007B/2704